AF200015

Impressum
Verlag: BABADADA GmbH, Nedderfeld 112 , 22529 Hamburg
Geschäftsführer / Verlagsleitung: Harald Hof
Druck: Books on Demand GmbH, In de Tarpen 42, 22848 Norderstedt

Imprint
Publisher: BABADADA GmbH, Nedderfeld 112 , 22529 Hamburg, Germany
Managing Director / Publishing direction: Harald Hof
Print: Books on Demand GmbH, In de Tarpen 42, 22848 Norderstedt

school

мактаб

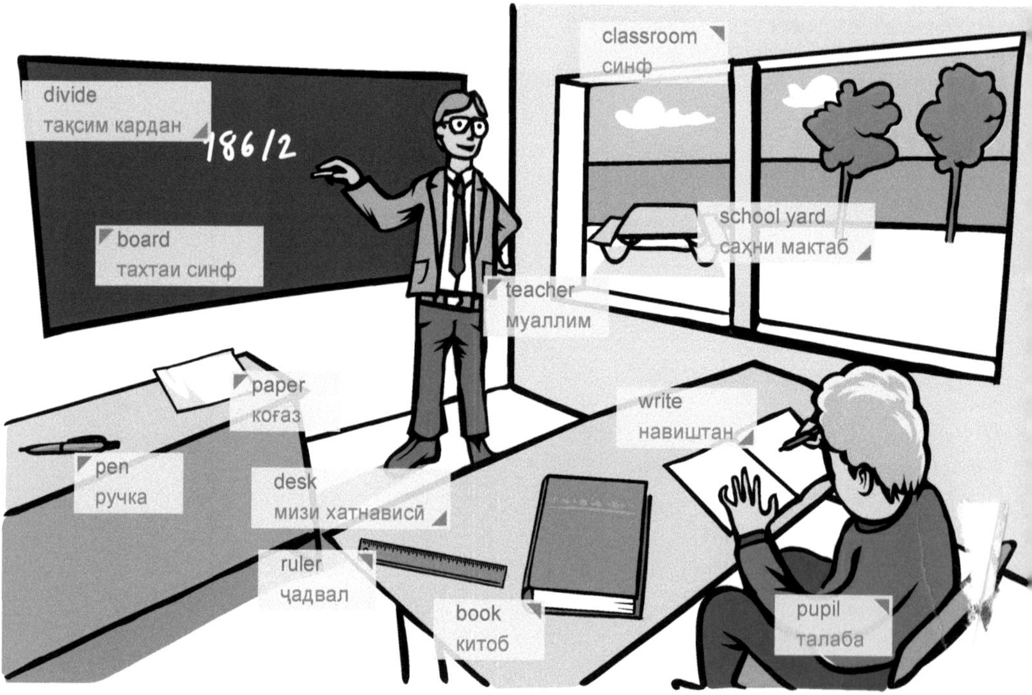

classroom
синф
divide
тақсим кардан
186/2
board
тахтаи синф
school yard
саҳни мактаб
teacher
муаллим
paper
коғаз
write
навиштан
pen
ручка
desk
мизи хатнависӣ
ruler
ҷадвал
book
китоб
pupil
талаба

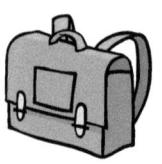

satchel

ҷузвдон

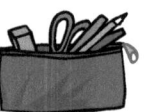

pencil case

қаламдон

pencil

қалам

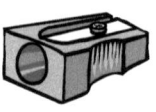

pencil sharpener

қаламтезкунак

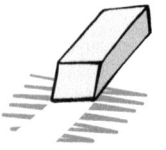

rubber

хаткуркунак

drawing pad

блокноти расмкашӣ

drawing

расм

paintbrush

мӯқалами рассомӣ

paint box

қуттии рангҳо

scissors

қайчӣ

glue

ширеш

exercise book

дафтари машқ

homework

вазифаи хонагӣ

number

рақам

add

ҷамъ кардан

subtract

кам кардан

multiply

зарб задан

calculate

ҳисоб кардан

letter

ҳарф

alphabet

алфавит

word

калима

text

матн

read

хондан

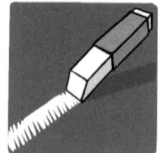

chalk

бӯр

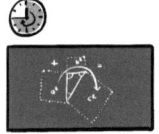

lesson

дарс

register

журнали синфӣ

exam

имтиҳон

certificate

шаҳодатнома

school uniform

либоси мактабӣ

education

таҳсил/маориф

encyclopedia

энсиклопедия

university

донишгоҳ

microscope

микроскоп (more frequently used)

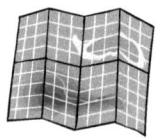

map

харита

waste-paper basket

сабади партофҳои коғазӣ

travel
саёҳат

hotel
меҳмонхона
Grand
hostel
хобгоҳ
ROOMS
EXCHANGE
bureau de change
нуқтаи мубодилаи асъор
car
мошин

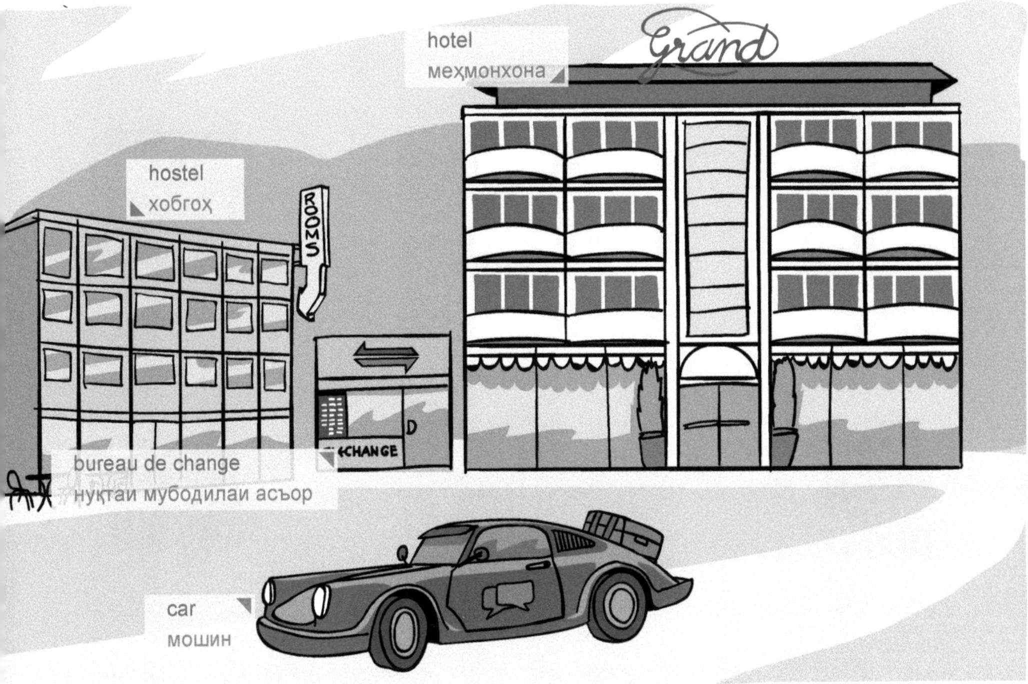

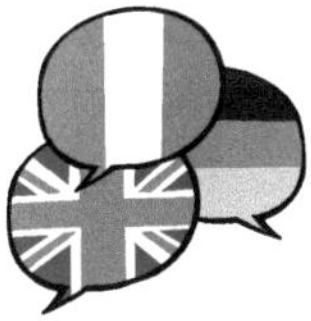

language
забон

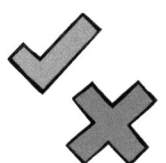

yes / no
ҳа / не

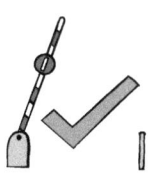

Okay
Хуб

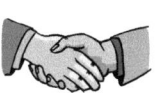

hello
Ассалому алейкум

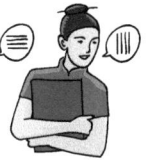

translator
тарҷумон

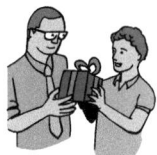

Thank you
Раҳмат

how much is...?

чӣ қадар аст ...?

I do not understand

Ман намефаҳмам

problem

проблема

Good evening!

шаб ба хайр!

Good morning!

субҳ ба хайр

Good night!

шаби хуш

bye bye

хайр

direction

равона

luggage

бағоҷ

bag

ҷузвдон

backpack

борхалта

guest

меҳмон

room

хона

sleeping bag

хобхалта

tent

хайма

tourist information

маълумоти сайёҳӣ

beach

соҳил

credit card

корти кредитӣ

breakfast

наҳорӣ

lunch

хӯроки пешин

dinner

хӯроки шом

ticket

чипта

lift

лифт

stamp

марка

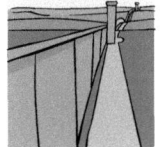

border

сарҳад

customs

Гумрук

embassy

сафорат

visa

раводид

passport

шиноснома

travel - саёҳат

transport
нақлиёт

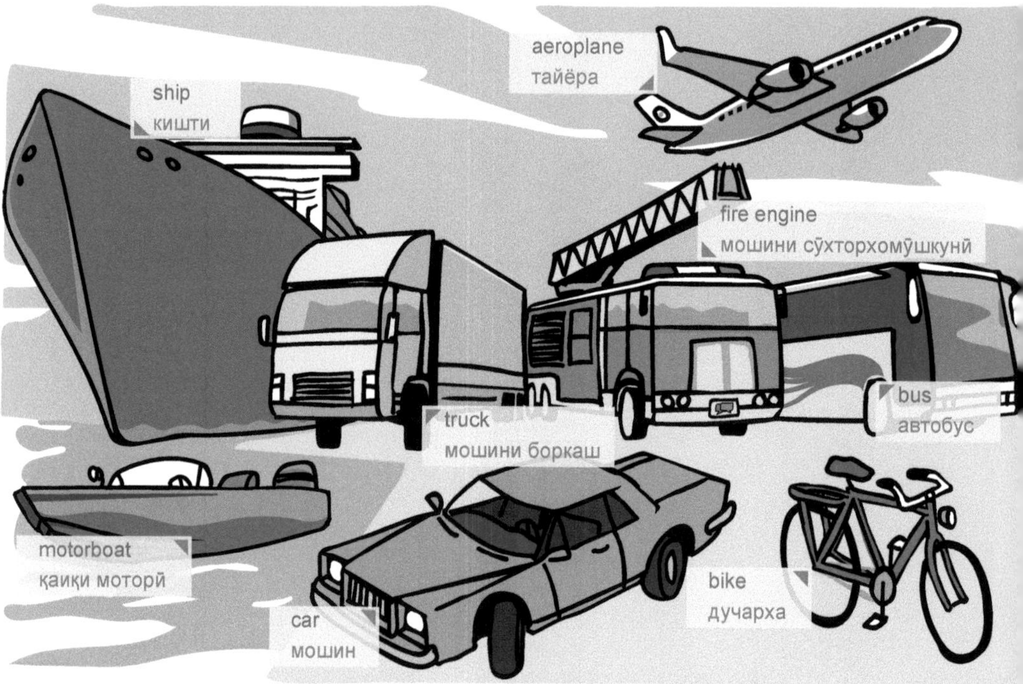
aeroplane
тайёра
ship
кишти
fire engine
мошини сӯхторхомӯшкунӣ
bus
автобус
truck
мошини боркаш
motorboat
қаиқи моторӣ
bike
дучарха
car
мошин

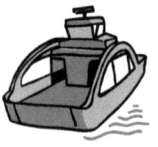

ferry

паром

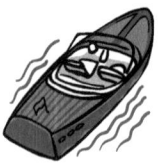

boat

қаиқ

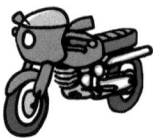

motorbike

мотосикл

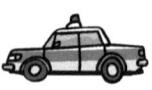

police car

мошини полис

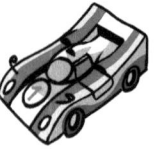

racing car

мошини тезрави пойгаи

rental car

кирояи мошинҳо

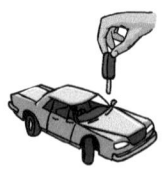

car sharing

ҳамроҳ истифодабарии мошин

breakdown truck

эвакуатор

refuse truck

павтовҷамъкунӣ

motor

муҳаррик

fuel

сӯзишворӣ

petrol station

нуқтаи фурӯши сӯзишворӣ

traffic sign

аломати роҳ

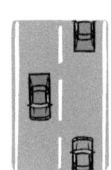

traffic

ҳаракат

traffic jam

бандшавии ҳаракати роҳ

car park

ҷои исти мошинҳо

train station

истгоҳи роҳи оҳан

tracks

роҳи оҳан

train

қатора

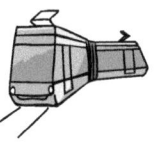

tram

тамвай

carriage

вагон

helicopter

чархбол

airport

фурудгоҳ

tower

манора

passenger

мусофир

container

контейнер

carton

қутии картонй

cart

ароба

basket

сабад

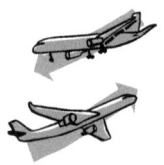

take off / land

гирифтан / замин

city

шаҳр

village

деҳа

city centre

маркази шаҳр

house

хона

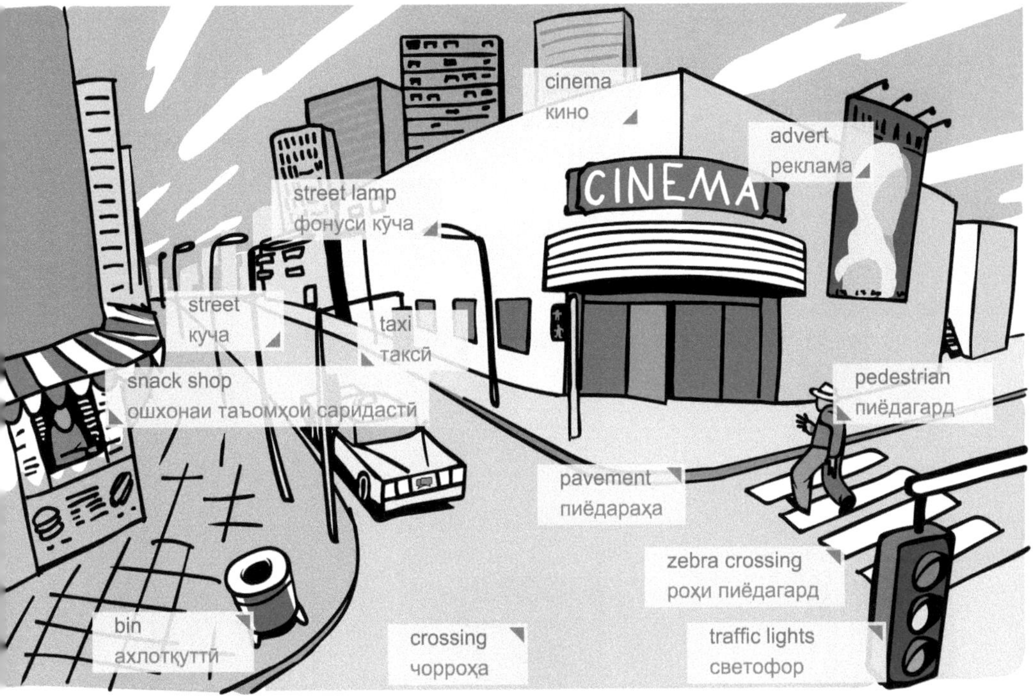
cinema
кино
advert
реклама
street lamp
фонуси кӯча
CINEMA
street
кӯча
taxi
таксӣ
snack shop
ошхонаи таъомҳои саридастӣ
pedestrian
пиёдагард
pavement
пиёдараҳа
zebra crossing
роҳи пиёдагард
bin
ахлотқуттӣ
crossing
чорроҳа
traffic lights
светофор

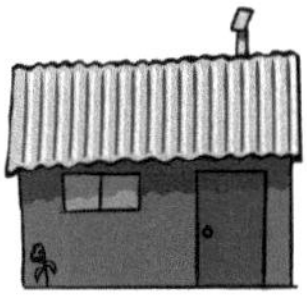

hut

кулба

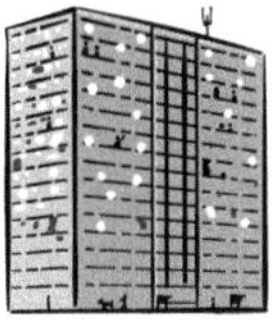

flat

ҳамвор

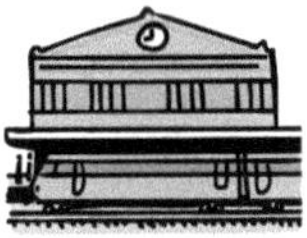

train station

истгоҳи роҳи оҳан

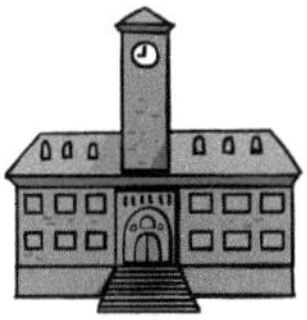

town hall

бинои маъмурияти шаҳр

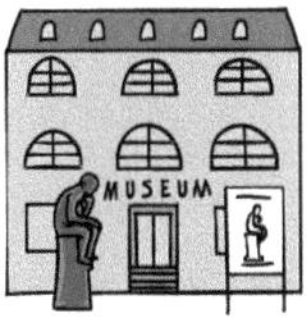
MUSEUM

museum

осорхона

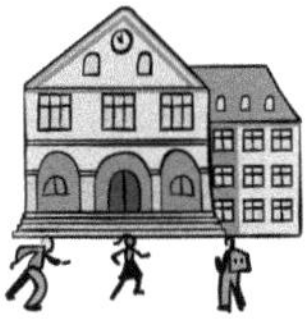

school

мактаб

university

донишгоҳ

bank

бонк

hospital

бемористон

hotel

меҳмонхона

pharmacy

доухона

office

идора

book shop

сеҳи китоб

shop

сеҳи

florist's

мағозаи гулфурӯшӣ

supermarket

супермаркет

market

бозор

department store

универмаг

fishmonger's

мағозаи моҳифурӯшӣ

shopping centre

маркази савдо

harbour

бандар

city - шаҳр

park

парк

bench

бонк

bridge

пул

stairs

зинапоя

underground

метро

tunnel

нақби

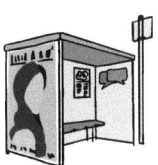

bus stop

истгоҳи автобус

bar

бар

restaurant

тарабхона

postbox

қуттии почта

street sign

аломати номи кӯчаҳо

parking meter

ҳисобкунаки исти мошинҳо

zoo

боғи ҳайвонот

swimming pool

ҳавзи шиноварӣ

mosque

масҷид

farm

ферма

pollution

ифлоскунӣ

graveyard

қабристон

church

калисо

playground

майдончаи бозӣ

temple

маъбад

landscape
ландшафт

signpost
аломати роҳнамо

way
роҳ

meadow
алафзор

stone
санг

hiker
сайёҳ

tree
дарахт

river
дарё

grass
алаф

flower
гул

valley

водй

hill

кӯҳ

lake

кул

forest

беша

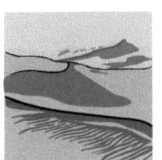

desert

биёбон

volcano

вулкан

castle

қалъа

rainbow

рангинкамон

mushroom

занбӯруғ

palm tree

дарати нахл

mosquito

хомӯшак

fly

паридан

ant

мурча

bee

занбур

spider

тортанак

landscape - ландшафт

15

beetle

гамбӯсак

frog

қурбоққа

squirrel

санҷоб

hedgehog

хорпушт

hare

харгӯш

owl

бум

bird

парранда

swan

мурғи қу

boar

хуки ваҳшӣ

deer

оху

moose

гавазн

dam

сарбанд

wind turbine

турбина шамол

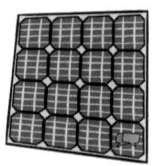

solar panel

панел офтобӣ

climate

иқлим

restaurant

тарабхона

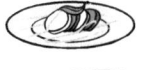

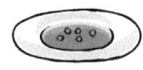

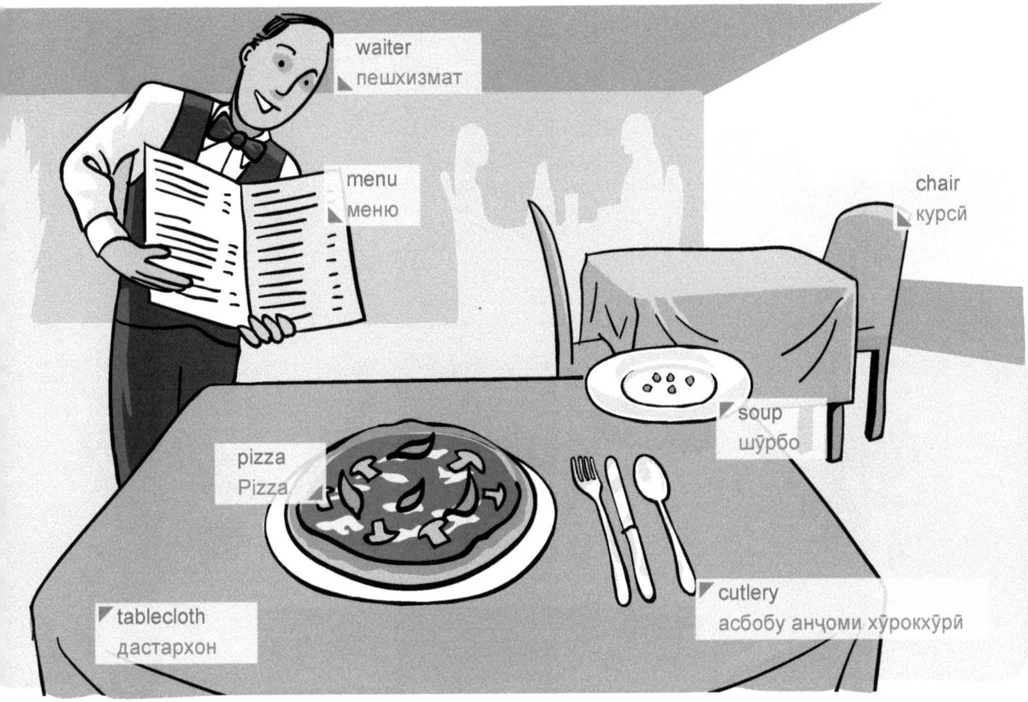

waiter
пешхизмат
menu
меню
chair
курсӣ
soup
шӯрбо
pizza
Pizza
tablecloth
дастархон
cutlery
асбобу анҷоми хӯрокхӯрӣ

starter
....
стартер/корандоз

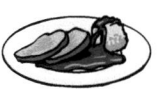

main course
....
хӯроки асосӣ

dessert
....
десерт

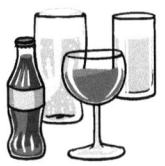

drinks
....
нӯшокиҳои

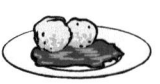

food
....
таъом

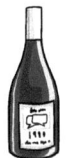

bottle
....
шиша

fast food

Хӯроки Тез Таёр мешуда

street food

хӯроки кӯчагӣ

teapot

чойник

sugar bowl

шакардон

portion

қисм/порча

espresso machine

мошини espresso

high chair

курсии кӯдакона

bill

ҳисоб

tray

зарфмонак

knife

корд

fork

чангол

spoon

қошуқ

teaspoon

қошуқча

serviette

сачоқи қоғазӣ

glass

истакон

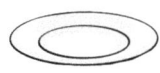

plate

табақча

soup plate

косача

saucer

тақсимча

sauce

соус

salt pot

намакдон

pepper mill

мурчдон

vinegar

сирко

oil

равғани растанӣ

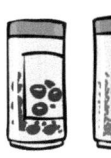

spices

приправа

ketchup

кетчуп

mustard

хардал

mayonnaise

майонез

supermarket
супермаркет

special offer
пешниҳоди махсус
FOR
customer
мизоҷ
dairy
шир
fruit
мева
trolley
аробача

BUTCHERS

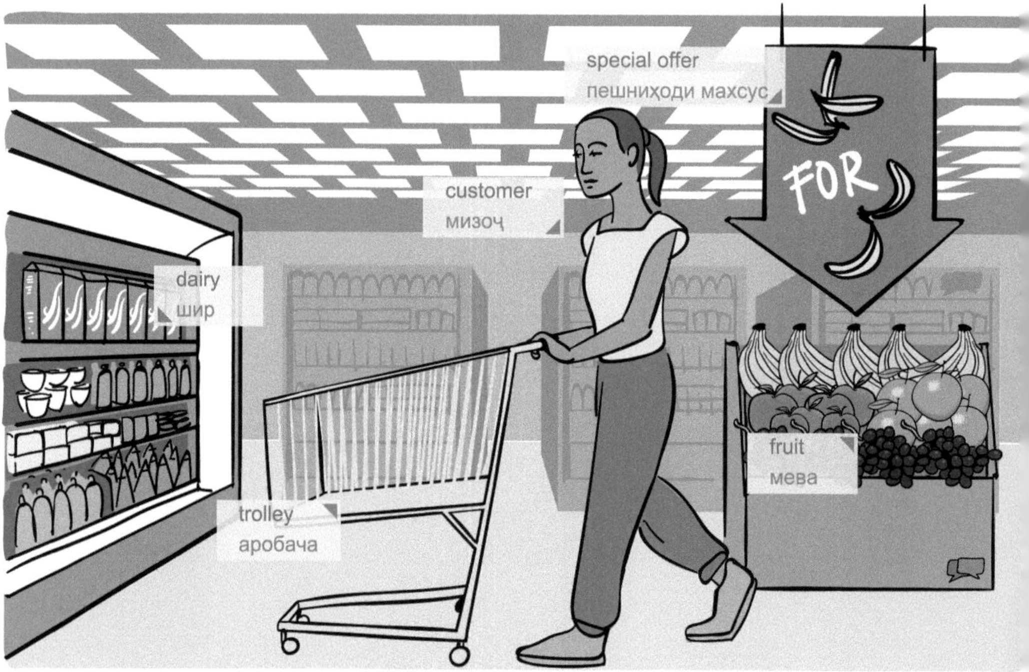

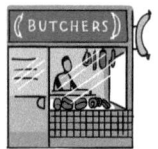

butcher´s
дукони гӯштфурӯшӣ

BAKERY

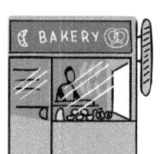

baker´s
дукони нонфурӯшӣ

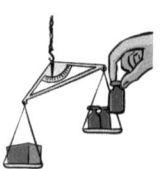

weigh
баркашидан

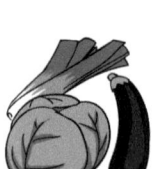

vegetables
сабзавот

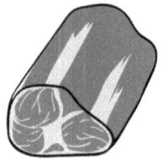

meat
гӯшт

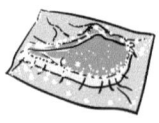

frozen food
хӯроки яхбаста

cold meat

тилимҳои борик буридаи гушт

tinned food

озуқаворӣ консервонидашуда

washing powder

хокаи либосшӯй

sweets

ширинӣ

household products

асбоби рӯзгор

cleaning products

воситаҳои тозакунанда

salesperson

фурӯшанда

till

касса

cashier

кассир

shopping list

рӯихати харидкунӣ

opening hours

соат ифтитоҳи

wallet

ҳамён

credit card

корти кредитӣ

bag

ҷуздо

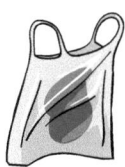

plastic bag

пакет

water

об

juice

шарбат

milk

шир

coke

кола

wine

шароб

beer

оби ҷав

alcohol

машрубот

cocoa

какао

tea

чой

coffee

қаҳва

espresso

эспрессо

cappuccino

каппучино

banana

банан

apple

себ

orange

норанҷй

melon

харбуза

lemon

лимӯ

carrot

сабзй

garlic

сир

bamboo

бамбук

onion

пиёз

mushroom

занбӯруғ

nuts

чормағз

noodles

угро

spaghetti

спагеттй

rice

биринҷ

salad

салат

chips

картошкаи қоқак

fried potatoes

картошкабирён

pizza

Pizza

hamburger

гамбургер

sandwich

бутербурод

cutlet

шнитсел

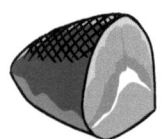

ham

гӯшти намакардаи хук

salami

ҳасиби салямй

sausage

ҳасиб

chicken

мурғ

roast

кабоб

fish

моҳй

porridge oats

ярмаи ҷав

muesli

омехтаи ғалладонагӣ

cornflakes

ярмаи ҷуворимакка

flour

орд

croissant

кулчақанд

bread roll

кулчақанд

bread

нон

toast

як порча нони бирён

biscuits

кулчачаҳои қандин

butter

маска

curd

творог

cake

пирог

egg

тухм

fried egg

тухм бирён

cheese

панир

ice cream

яхмос

sugar

шакар

honey

асал

jam

мураббо

chocolate spread

хамираи ҳалво

curry

Curry

food - таъом

goat

буз

cow

гов

calf

гӯсола

pig

хук

piglet

хукча

bull

буққа

goose

қоз

duck

мурғобӣ

chick

чӯча

hen

мурғ

cock

хурӯс

rat

каламуш

cat

гурба

mouse

муш

ox

барзагов

dog

саг

doghouse

хоначаи саг

garden hose

рӯдаи резинӣ

watering can

камобӣ метавонад

scythe

дос

plough

сипори шудгоркунии замин

sickle

доси

hoe

каланд

pitchfork

панҷшоха

axe

табар

wheelbarrow

ароба

trough

охур

milk can

зарфи ширгирӣ

sack

халта

fence

девор

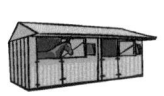

stable

мӯътадил

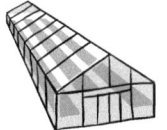

greenhouse

гармхона

soil

хок

seed

тухмӣ

fertilizer

нуриҳо

combine harvester

комбайни ғаллағундорӣ

harvest

ҳосил

harvest

ҳосил

yams

yams

wheat

гандум

soy

лубиж

potato

картошка

corn

ҷуворӣ

rapeseed

донаи маъсар

fruit tree

дарахти мева

cassava

manioc

cereals

ғалладона

living room

мехмонхона

bathroom

ҳамом

kitchen

ошхона

bedroom

хонаи хоб

child's room

хучраи кӯдакона

dining room

ошхона

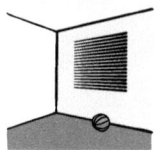

floor

ошёна

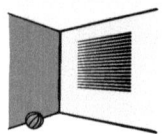

wall

девор

ceiling

шифт

cellar

тагзаминӣ

sauna

сауна

balcony

балкон

terrace

суфача

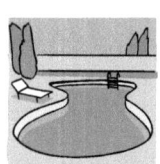

pool

ҳавз

lawn mower

мошини алафдарав

sheet

варақ

bedspread

кампал

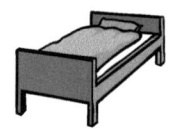

bed

кат

broom

ҷорӯб

bucket

сатил

switch

калид

living room
мехмонхона

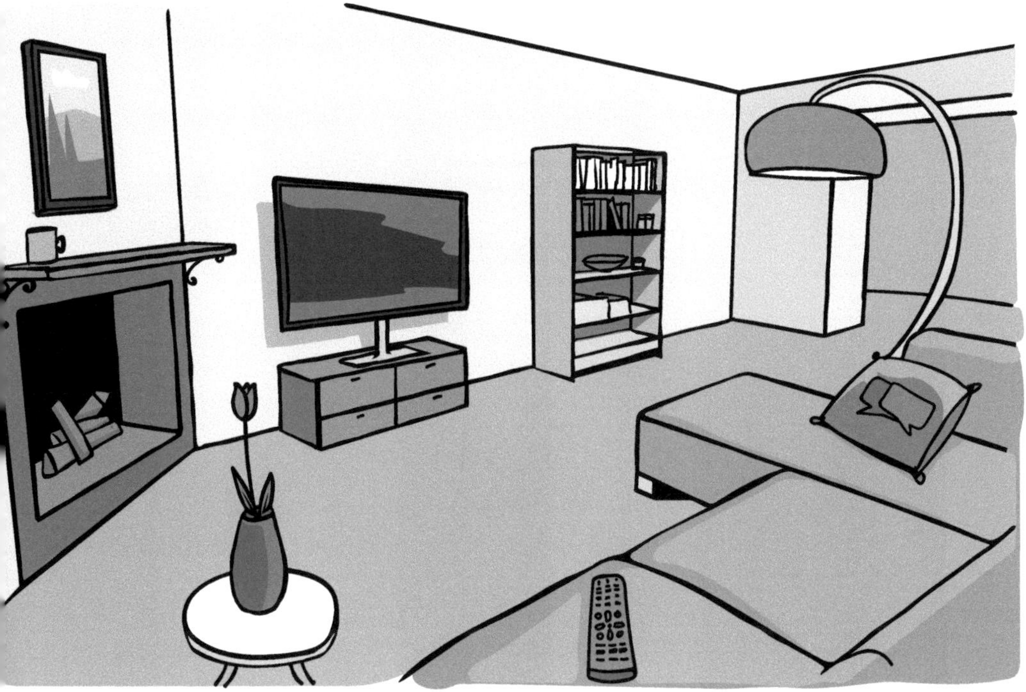

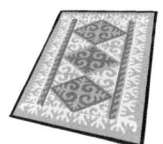

carpet

қолин

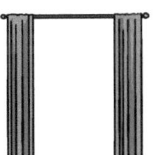

curtain

парда

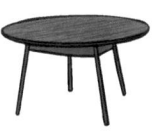

table

мизи

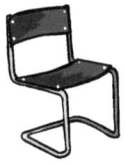

chair

курсӣ

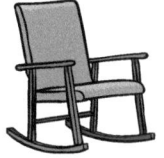

rocking chair

rocking кафедраи

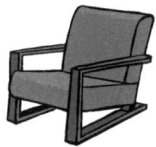

armchair

курсӣ

book

китоб

blanket

курпа

decoration

ороиш

firewood

ҳезум

film

филм

hi-fi equipment

дастгоҳи hi-fi

key

калид

newspaper

рӯзнома

painting

расм

poster

эълон

radio

радио

notepad

китобчаи қайдҳо

hoover

чангкашак

cactus

кактус

candle

шам

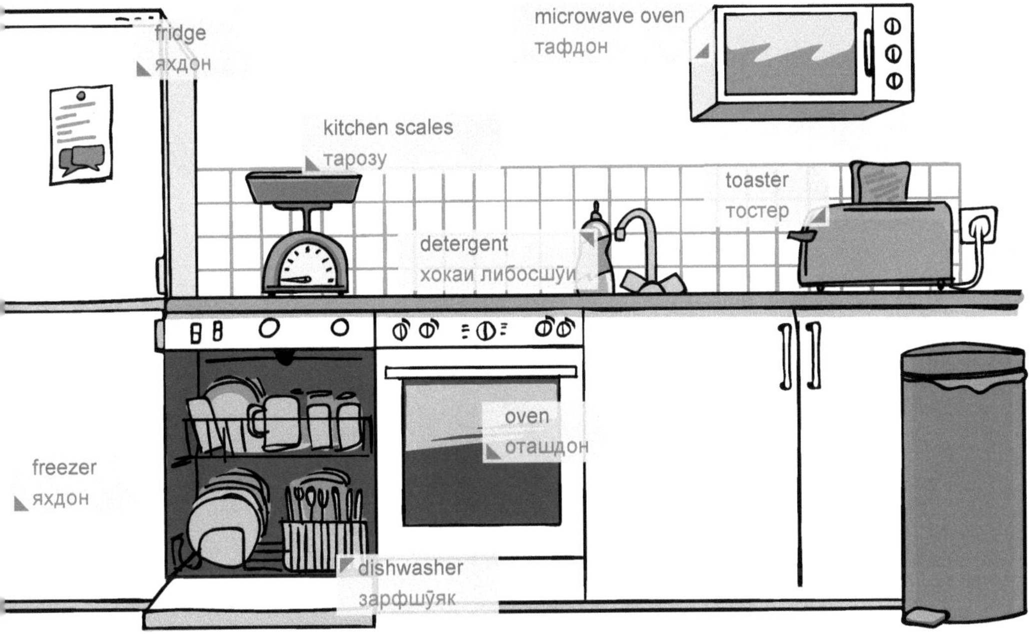

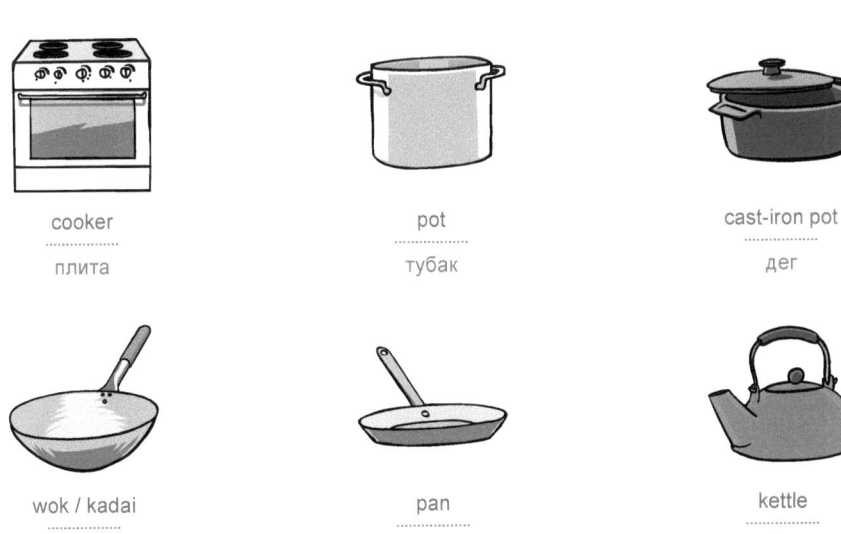

fridge
яхдон

microwave oven
тафдон

kitchen scales
тарозу

detergent
хокаи либосшӯи

toaster
тостер

oven
оташдон

freezer
яхдон

dishwasher
зарфшӯяк

cooker
плита

pot
тубак

cast-iron pot
дег

wok / kadai
дег / кадй

pan
тоба

kettle
чойник

steamer

steamer

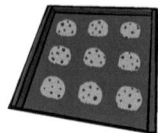

baking tray

лист

crockery

зарф

mug

кружка

bowl

коса

chopsticks

чубаки хурокхӯрӣ

ladle

кафлези

spatula

кафлези ҳамвор

whisk

whisk

strainer

strainer

sieve

элак

grater

турбтарошак

mortar

миномет

barbecue

Кабоб Кардан

open fire

оташ кушод

chopping board

тахтаи резакунӣ

rolling pin

чӯба

corkscrew

пӯккашак

can

банка

can opener

консервокушояк

pot holder

дастак

sink

дастшӯяк

brush

чӯтка

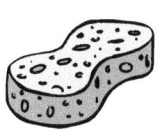

sponge

исфанҷ

blender

блендер

deep freezer

сармодон

baby bottle

шишача

tap

чумак

bathroom

ҳамом

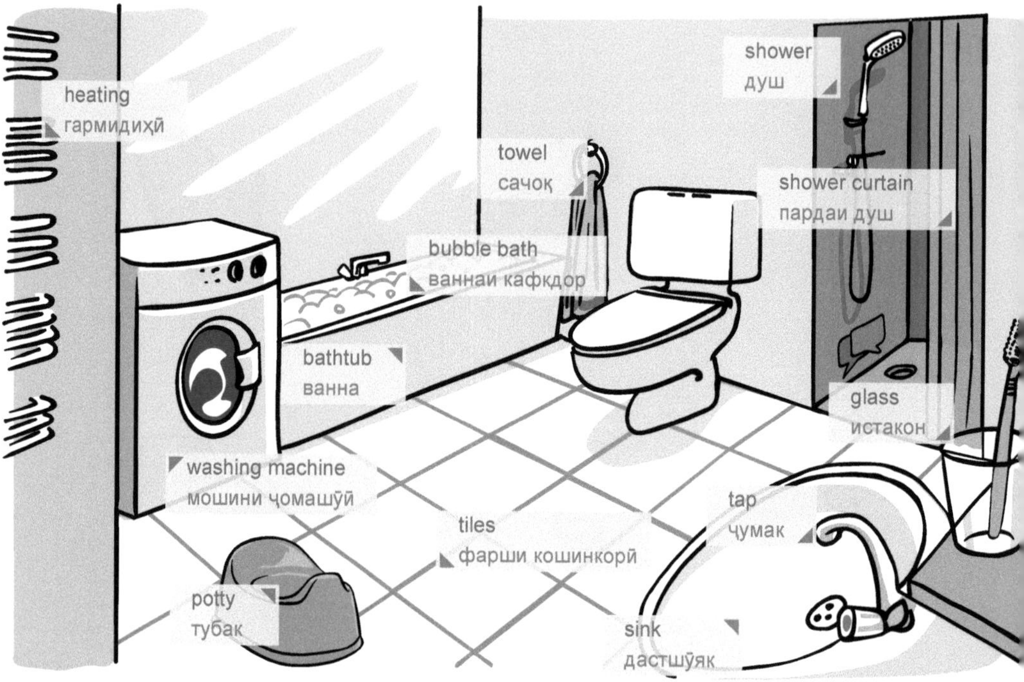

heating
гармидиҳӣ
towel
сачоқ
shower
душ
shower curtain
пардаи душ
bubble bath
ваннаи кафкдор
bathtub
ванна
glass
истакон
washing machine
мошини ҷомашӯӣ
tap
ҷумак
tiles
фарши кошинкорӣ
potty
тубак
sink
дастшӯяк

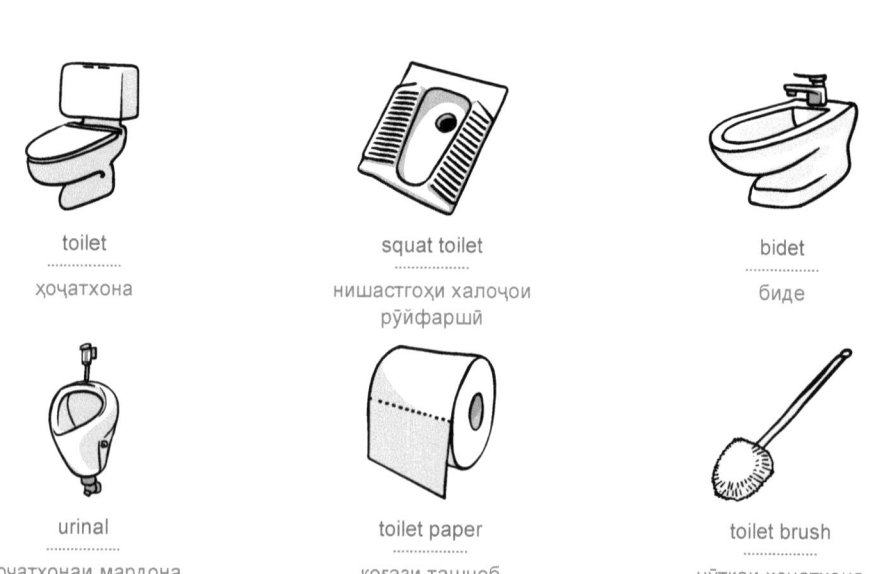

toilet

ҳоҷатхона

squat toilet

нишастгоҳи халоҷои руйфаршӣ

bidet

биде

urinal

ҳоҷатхонаи мардона

toilet paper

коғази ташноб

toilet brush

чӯткаи ҳоҷатхона

toothbrush

дандоншӯяк

toothpaste

хамираи дандоншӯи

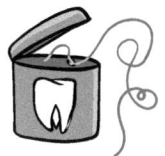

dental floss

риштаи дандонтозакунӣ

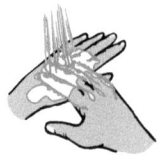

wash

шӯстан

handheld shower

души дастӣ

douche

обшӯй

basin

ҳавза

back brush

шона кардани мӯй

soap

собун

shower gel

гел барои душ

shampoo

шампун

flannel

бумазӣ

drain

заҳкаш

cream

крем

deodorant

дезодорант

mirror

оина

hand mirror

оинаи дастй

razor

риштарошаки барқи

shaving foam

кафк барои риштарошй

aftershave

оби мушкини баъди риштарошй

comb

шона

brush

чӯтка

hair dryer

мӯйхушкунак

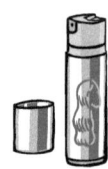

hairspray

лак барои мӯй

makeup

косметика

lipstick

лабсурхкунак

nail varnish

лок барои нохун

cotton wool

пахта

nail scissors

қайчии нохунгирй

perfume

атриёт

washbag

ҷузвдони косметики

stool

қазои ҳоҷат

weighing scale

тарозу

bathrobe

хилъат

rubber gloves

дастпӯшак резина

tampon

тампон

sanitary towel

дастмоли санитарӣ

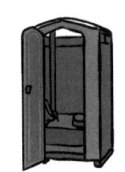

chemical toilet

био-ҳоҷатхона

child's room

ҳуҷраи кӯдакона

alarm clock
соати рӯимизии зангдор
cuddly toy
бозичаи мулоим
toy car
мошини бозича
rattle
тиқ-тиқ кардан
doll's house
хоначаи бозичагӣ
present
ҳузур

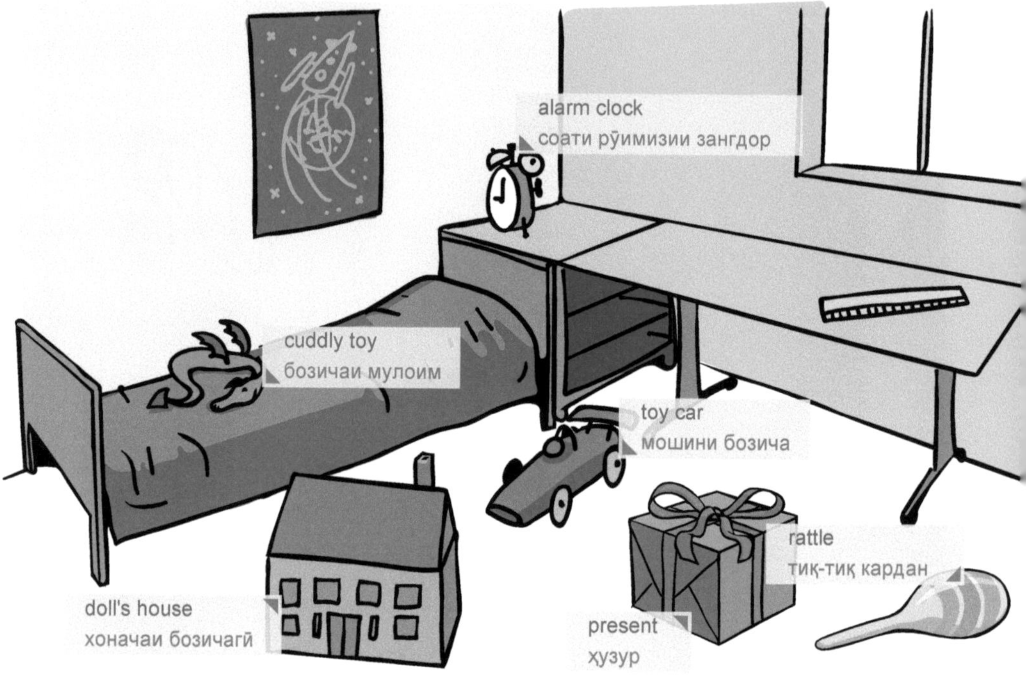

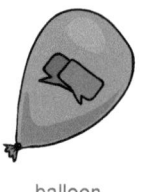

balloon

пуфак

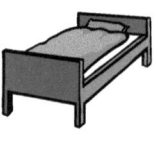

bed

кат

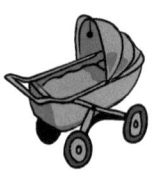

pram

аробочаи кудакона

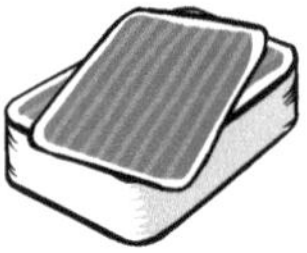

deck of cards

маҷмӯи кортҳо

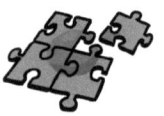

jigsaw

бозии муамоёбӣ

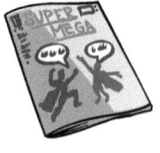

comic

комикс

lego bricks

хиштҳои лего

building blocks

мағозаи бозичафурӯхтан

action figure

рақам амал

babygrow

либоси ғаваккашӣ

frisbee

фрисби

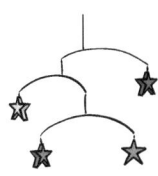

mobile

мобилӣ

board game

лавҳачаи бозӣ

dice

кубик

model train set

маҷмӯи модели қатора

dummy

пистонак

party

ҳизб

picture book

китоби расм

ball

тӯб

doll

лӯхтак

play

бози кардан

sandpit

қуттии рег

swing

арғунчак

toys

бозича

video game console

консоли бозиҳои видеой

tricycle

велосипеди сечарха

teddy bear

хирсаки бахмалии патдор

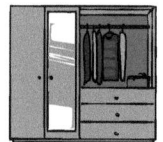

wardrobe

ҷевон

clothing

либос

socks

ҷуроб

stockings

ҷуроби соқбаланд

tights

колготки

scarf
гарданпеч

belt
тасма

umbrella
чатр

t-shirt
футболка

trainers
кроссовки

boots
пойафзол

slippers
шиппак

sandals
босоножкй

shoes
пойафзол

rubber boots
музаи резинй

underpants
турсй

bra
синабанд

vest
майка

body

бадан

trousers

шим

jeans

чинс

skirt

юбка

blouse

куртаи нимтаи занона

shirt

курта

pullover

свитер

hoodie

свитер

blazer

пичак

jacket

нимтана

coat

палто

raincoat

плаш

costume

костюм

dress

куртаи занона

wedding dress

либос тӯйи

suit

костюм

nightgown

куртаи хоб

pyjamas

пижама

sari

Сари

headscarf

рӯймол

turban

салла

burqa

ниқобу

kaftan

кафтан

abaya

абая

swimsuit

либоси обозӣ

trunks

эзорчаи шиноварии мардона

shorts

шорти

tracksuit

либоси варзишӣ

apron

пешбанд

gloves

дастпӯшак

button
тугма

glasses
айнак

bracelet
дастпона

necklace
гарданбанд

ring
ангуштарин

earring
гӯшвора

cap
кулоҳ

coat hanger
либосовезак

hat
кулоҳ

tie
галстук

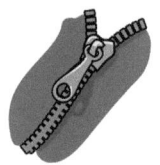

zip
занҷирак

helmet
тоскулоҳ

braces
шимбардор

school uniform
либоси мактабй

uniform
либоси

bib

пешгир

dummy

пистонак

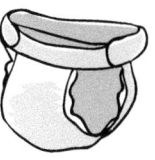

nappy

подгузник

office

идора

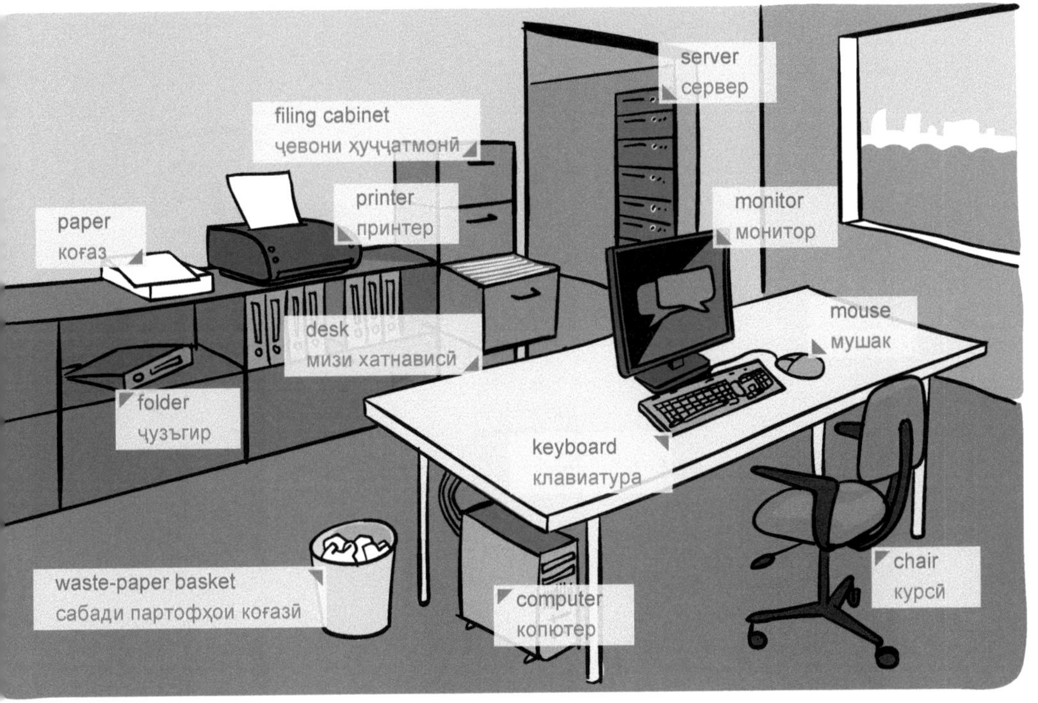

filing cabinet
чевони хуччатмонӣ

server
сервер

printer
принтер

monitor
монитор

paper
коғаз

mouse
мушак

desk
мизи хатнависӣ

folder
чузъгир

keyboard
клавиатура

waste-paper basket
сабади партофҳои коғазӣ

chair
курсӣ

computer
копютер

coffee mug

кружкаи қаҳванӯшӣ

calculator

калкулятор

internet

интернет

laptop

ноутбук

letter

мактуб

message

хабар

mobile

телефони мобилӣ

network

шабака

photocopier

нусхабардор

software

нармафзор

telephone

телефон

plug socket

розетка

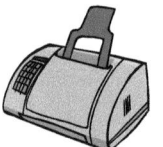

fax machine

факс

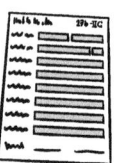

form

шакл

document

ҳуҷҷат

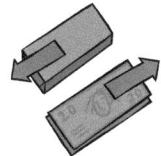

buy

харидан

pay

пардохт

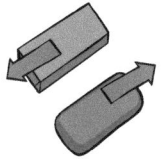

trade

савдо

money

пул

 **USD**

dollar

доллар

 **EUR**

euro

евро

 **JPY**

yen

йен

 **RUB**

rouble

рубл

 **CHF**

Swiss franc

франки швейцариягӣ

 **CNY**

renminbi yuan

юан

 **INR**

rupee

рупй

cashpoint

нуқтаи нақд

bureau de change

нуқтаи мубодилаи асъор

gold

тилло

silver

нуқра

oil

равғани растанӣ

energy

энерги

price

нарх

contract

шартнома

tax

андоз

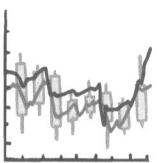

stock

саҳмия

work

кор

employee

хизматчӣ

employer

соҳибкор

factory

завод

shop

сехи

occupations
касбҳо

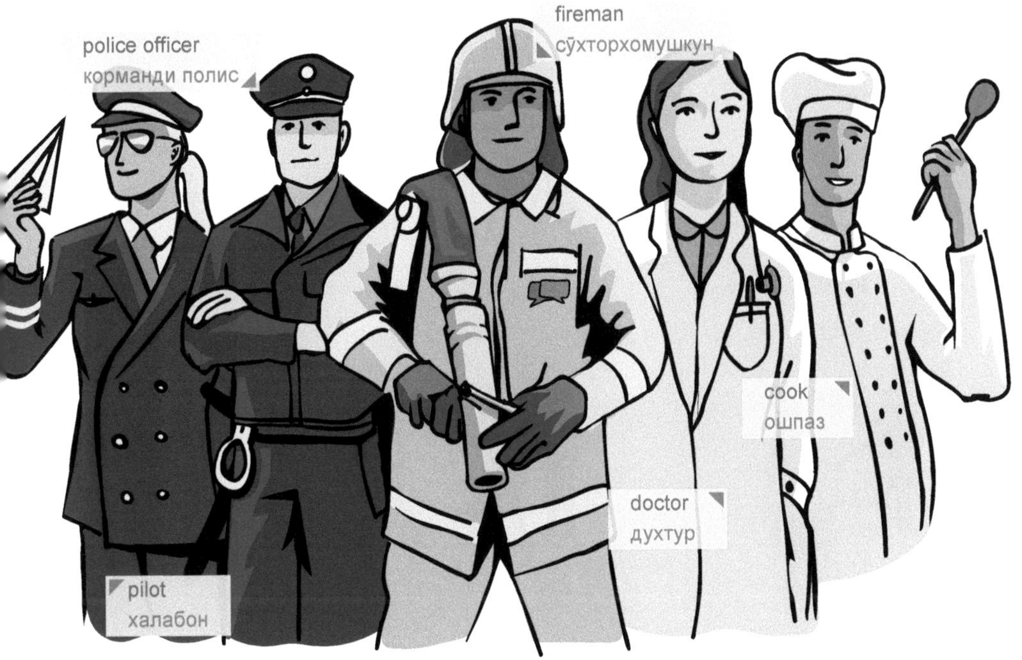
police officer
корманди полис
fireman
сўхторхомушкун
cook
ошпаз
doctor
духтур
pilot
халабон

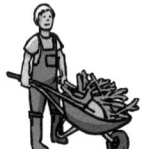

gardener
....
боғбон

carpenter
....
чўбтарош

seamstress
....
дўзанда

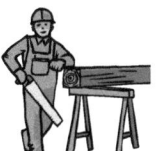

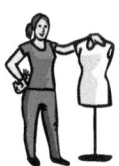

judge
....
судя

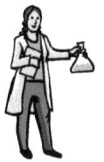

chemist
....
кимиёшинос

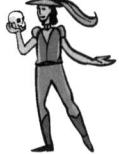

actor
....
актер

bus driver

ронандаи автобус

taxi driver

таксист

fisherman

моҳигир

cleaning lady

фаррошзан

roofer

устои бомпӯш

waiter

пешхизмат

hunter

шикорчӣ

painter

расом

baker

нонвой

electrician

барқ

builder

сохтмончӣ

engineer

инженер

butcher

қассоб

plumber

устои шабакаи об

postman

хаткашон

soldier

сарбоз

architect

меъмор

cashier

кассир

florist

гулфурӯш

hairdresser

сартарош

conductor

кондуктор

mechanic

механик

captain

капатан

dentist

духтури дандон

scientist

олим

rabbi

хохом

imam

имом

monk

шайх

clergyman

саркоҳин

tools
асбобҳо

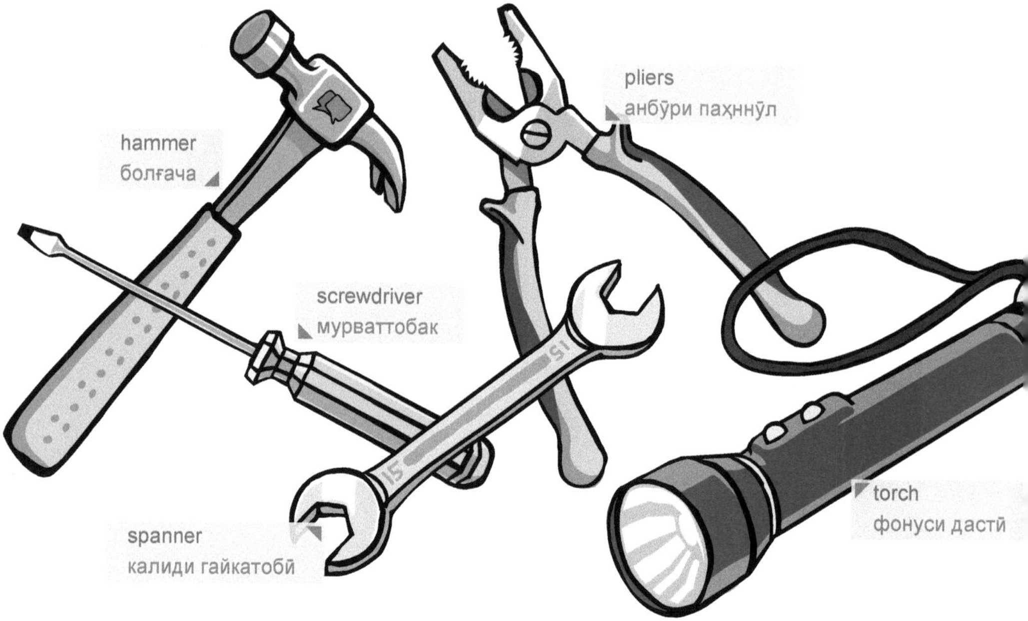

hammer
болғача
pliers
анбӯри паҳннӯл
screwdriver
мурваттобак
spanner
калиди гайкатобӣ
torch
фонуси дастӣ

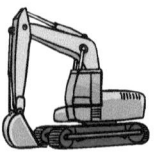

digger
экскаватор

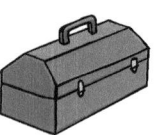

toolbox
қутии асбобҳо

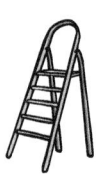

ladder
зинапоя

saw
арра

nails
мехҳо

drill
пармаи электрикӣ

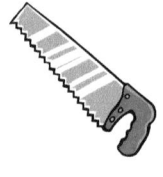

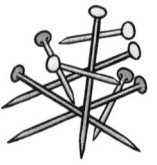

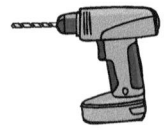

repair

таъмир

shovel

бел

Damn!

Сабил монад!

dustpan

белчаи хокрӯбагирӣ

paint pot

сатили ранг

screws

мехи печдор

musical instruments
асбобҳои мусиқӣ

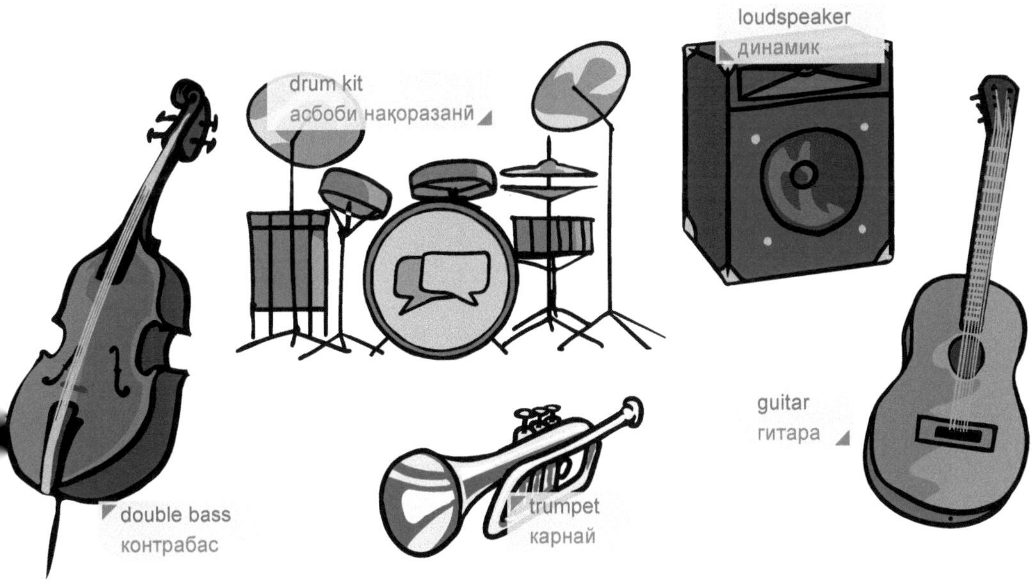

loudspeaker
динамик

drum kit
асбоби нақоразанӣ

double bass
контрабас

trumpet
карнай

guitar
гитара

piano
пианино

violin
ғиҷҷак

bass
бас-гитара

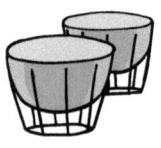

timpani
нақораи поядор

drums
нақора

keyboard
клавиатура

saxophone
саксофон

flute
най

microphone
баландгӯяд

tiger
паланг

entrance
даромад

cage
қафас

zebra
гӯрхар

animal feed
хӯроки чорво

panda
панда

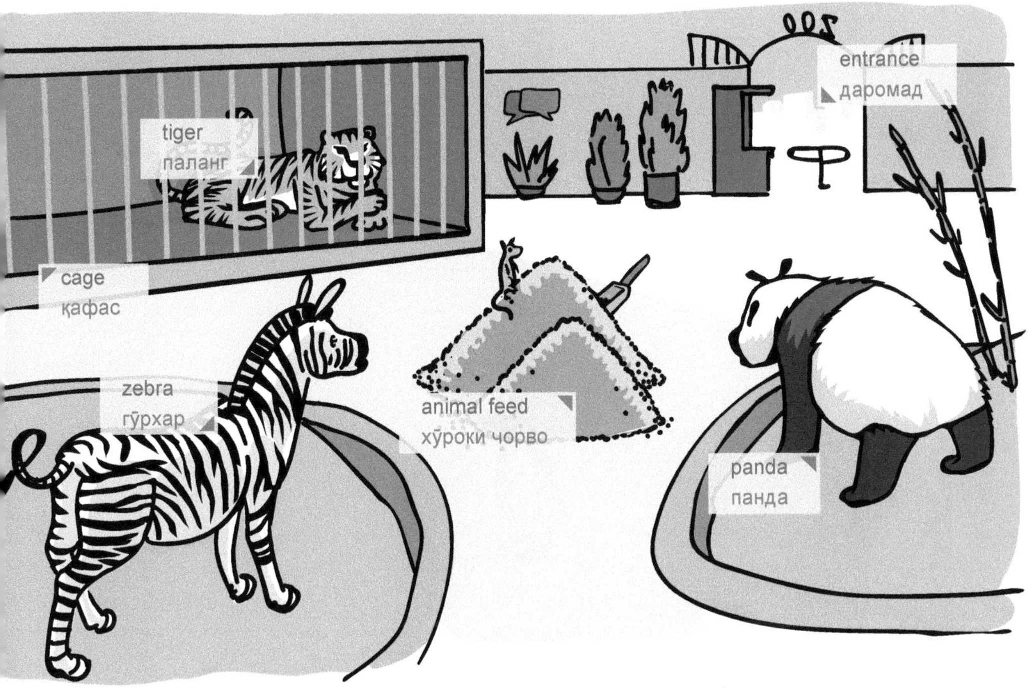

animals

ҳайвонот

elephant

фил

kangaroo

кенгуру

rhino

каркадан

gorilla

горилла

bear

хирси бӯр

camel

шутур

ostrich

шутурмурғ

lion

шер

monkey

маймун

flamingo

бутимор

parrot

тӯти

polar bear

хирси сафед

penguin

пингвин

shark

наҳанг

peacock

товус

snake

мор

crocodile

тимсоҳ

zookeeper

посбон

seal

сил

jaguar

ягуар

zoo - боғи ҳайвонот

pony

аспи кӯтоҳқад

leopard

леопард

hippo

баҳмут

giraffe

заррофа

eagle

уқоб

boar

хуки ваҳшӣ

fish

моҳӣ

turtle

сангпушт

walrus

морж

fox

рӯбоҳ

gazelle

ғизол/оху

sports
варзиш

American football
футболи амрикои

cycling
велосипедронӣ

tennis
теннис

basketball
баскетбол

swimming
шиноварӣ

boxing
бокс

ice hockey
хоккей

football
футбол

badminton
бадмингтон

athletics
атлетика

handball
гандбол

skiing
лижаронӣ

polo
тӯббозӣ бо асп

laugh
ханда

jump
паридан

hug
оғӯш гирифтан

walk
пиёда рафтан

sing
шеър хондан

dream
орзӯ кардан

pray
ибодат кардан

kiss
бӯса кардан

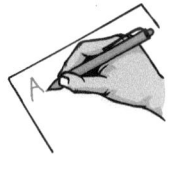

write

навиштан

draw

кашидан

show

нишон додан

push

тела додан

give

додан

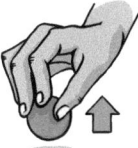

take

гирифтан

have

доранд

do

кор

be

бошад

stand

истодан

run

давидан

pull

кашидан

throw

партофтан

fall

афтидан

lie

дароз кашидан

wait

интизор шудан

carry

бардошта бурдан

sit

нишастан

get dressed

либос пӯшидан

sleep

хобин

wake up

бедор шудан

look at

нигоҳ кардан

cry

гиря кардан

stroke

сила кардан

comb

шона

talk

гап задан

understand

фаҳмидан

ask

пурсидан

listen

гӯш кардан

drink

нӯштдан

eat

хӯрдан

tidy up

ғундоштан

love

ишқ

cook

ошпаз

drive

рондан

fly

парвоз кардан

activities - фаъолият

sail

бо бодбон ҳаракат кардан

calculate

ҳисоб кардан

read

хондан

learn

омӯхтан

work

кор

marry

оиладор шудан

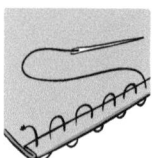

sew

дӯхтан

brush teeth

дадон шӯстан

kill

куштан

smoke

дуд

send

фиристодан

grandmother
биби

grandfather
бобо

father
падар

mother
модар

baby
кӯдак

daughter
хоҳар

son
писар

guest

меҳмон

aunt

хола

uncle

амак

brother

бародар

sister

хоҳар

body

бадан

forehead
пешонӣ
eye
чашм
shoulder
китф
finger
ангушт
face
рӯй
chin
манаҳ
hand
панҷаи даст
leg
пой
breast
қафаси сина
arm
даст

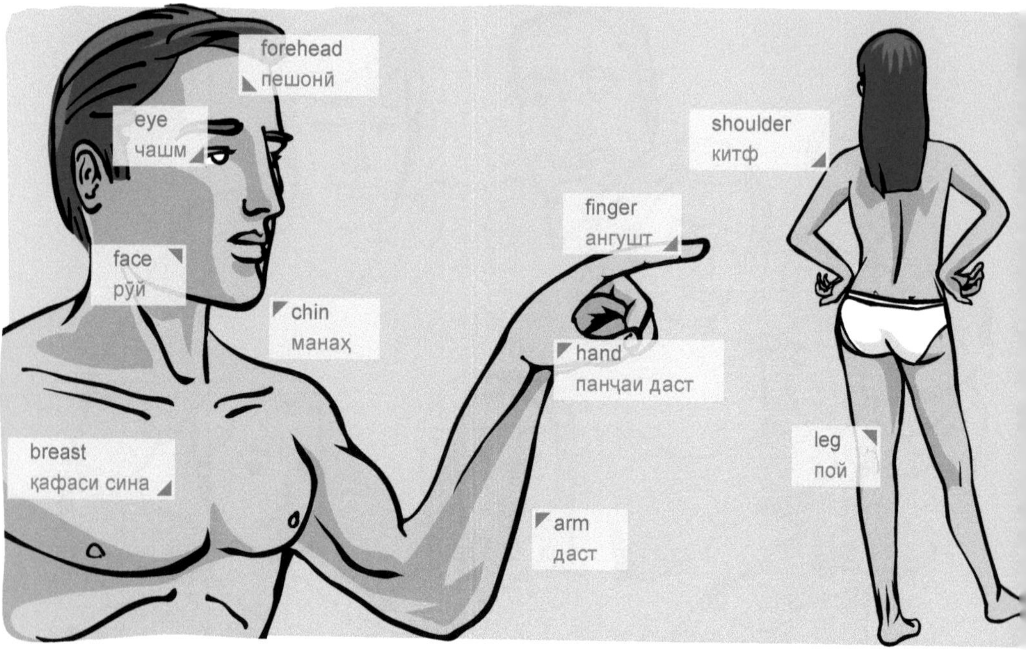

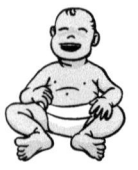

baby

кӯдак

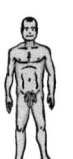

man

мард

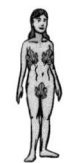

woman

зан

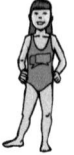

girl

духтар

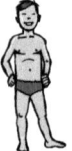

boy

писар

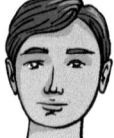

head

сар

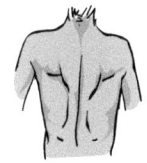

back

пушт

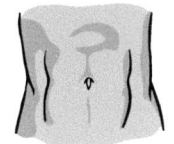

belly

шикам

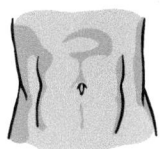

belly button

ноф

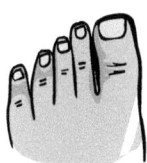

toe

ангушти пой

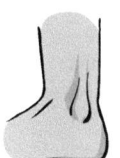

heel

пошнаи пой

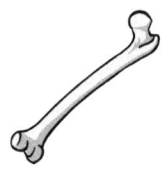

bone

устухон

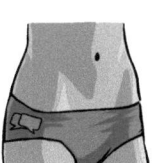

hip

рон

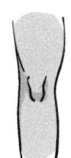

knee

зону

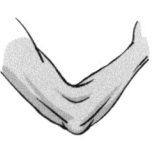

elbow

оринҷ

nose

бинй

bottom

таг

skin

пӯст

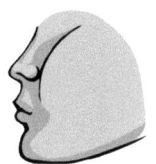

cheek

рухсора

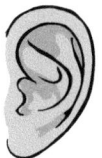

ear

гӯш

lip

лаб

body - бадан

mouth

даҳон

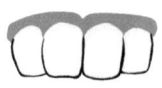

tooth

дадон

tongue

забон

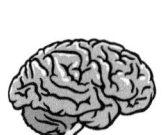

brain

майнаи сар

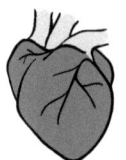

heart

дил

muscle

мушак

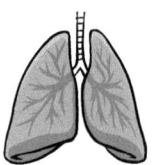

lung

шуш

liver

ҷигар

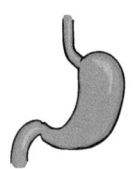

stomach

меъда

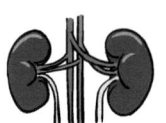

kidneys

гурдаҳо

sex

алоқаи ҷинсӣ

condom

рифола

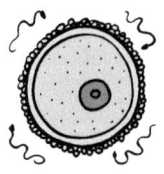

ovum

тухмҳуҷайра

semen

нутфа

pregnancy

ҳомиладорӣ

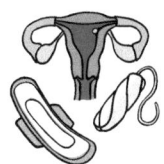

menstruation

ҳайз

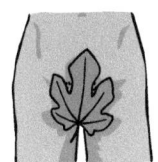

vagina

маҳбал

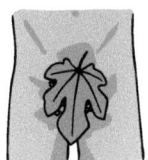

penis

кер

eyebrow

абрӯ

hair

мӯй

neck

гардан

hospital
бемористон

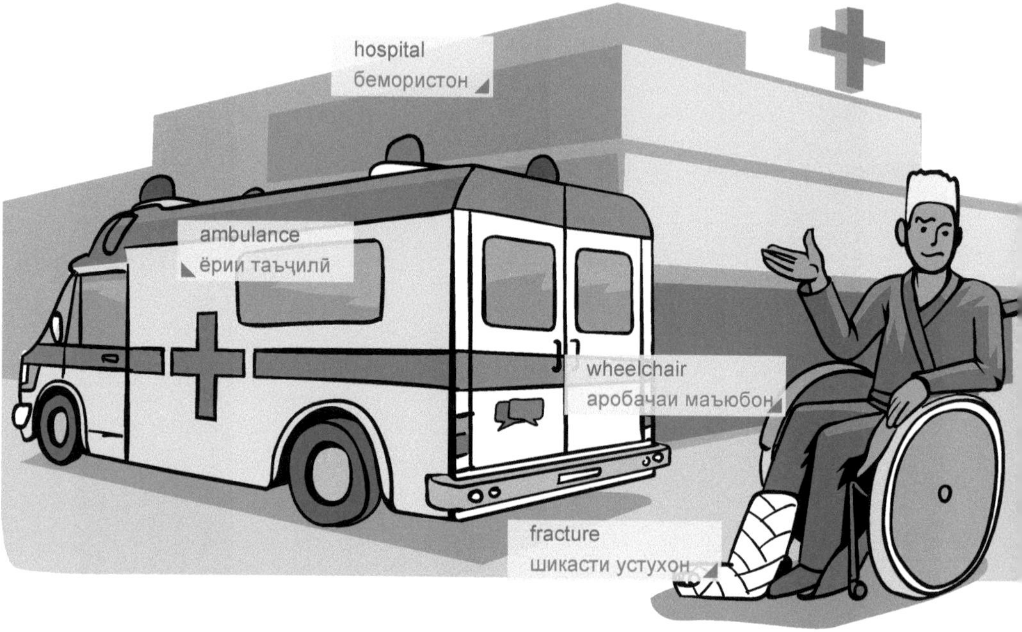
hospital
бемористон
ambulance
ёрии таъҷилӣ
wheelchair
аробачаи маъюбон
fracture
шикасти устухон

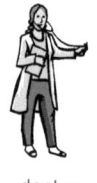

doctor
....
духтур

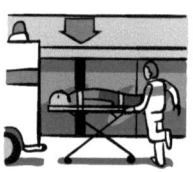

emergency room
....
ҳуҷраи ёрии фаврӣ

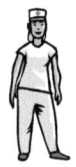

nurse
....
ҳамшираи тиббӣ

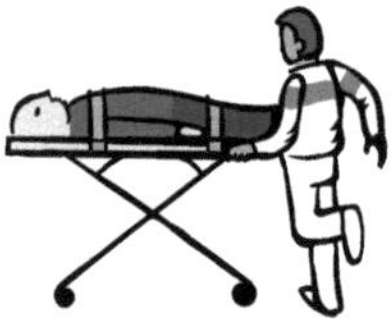

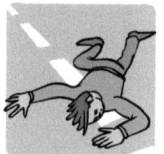

emergency
....
ҳолати фавқулодда

unconscious
....
беҳуш

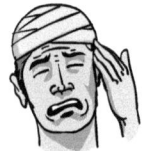

pain
....
дард

injury

чароҳат

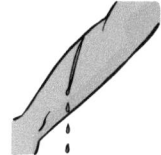

bleeding

хунравӣ

heart attack

дилзанак

stroke

сактаи майна

allergy

аллергия

cough

сулфа

fever

табларза

flu

грипп

diarrhoea

шикамравӣ

headache

сардард

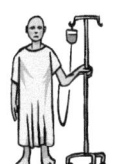

cancer

саратон

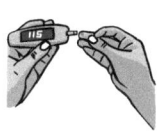

diabetes

диабет

surgeon

ҷарроҳ

scalpel

скалпел

operation

ҷарроҳӣ

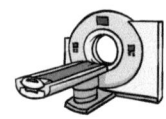

CT

Томографияи компютерй

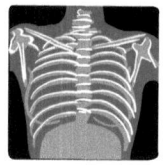

x-ray

шӯъои ренгенй

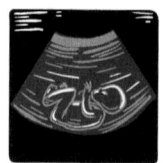

ultrasound

ултрасадо

face mask

ниқоби рӯй

disease

беморй

waiting room

ҳучраи интизорй

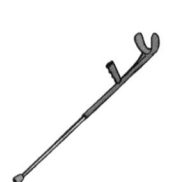

crutch

асобағал

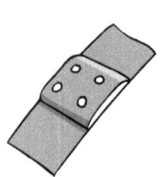

plaster

марҳам

bandage

дока

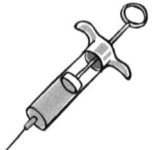

injection

сӯзандору

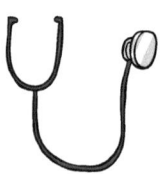

stethoscope

стетоскоп

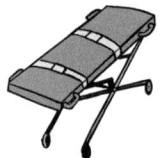

stretcher

занбар

clinical thermometer

ҳароратсанҷ

birth

таваллуд

overweight

вазни зиёдатй

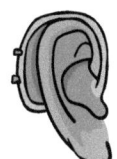

hearing aid

тачҳизоти шунавой

disinfectant

моддаи безараргардонй

infection

инфексия

virus

вирус

HIV / AIDS

ВИЧ / СПИД

medicine

дору

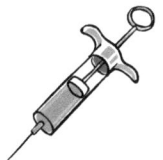

vaccination

ваксинатсия

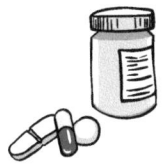

tablets

ҳабҳо

pill

ҳаб

emergency call

занги изтирорй

blood pressure monitor

монитори фишори хун

ill / healthy

бемор/солим

Help!

Кумак!

assault

ҳуҷум

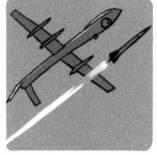

attack

ҳамла

danger

хатар

emergency exit

баромадгоҳи таҳлиявӣ

Fire!

Сӯхтор!

fire extinguisher

оташнишон

accident

садама

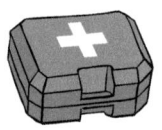

first-aid kit

дорукуттӣ

SOS

бонги хатар

police

полис

alarm

ҳушдор

Europe

Аврупо

North America

Америкаи Шимолй

South America

Америкаи Ҷанубй

Africa

Африка

Asia

Осиё

Australia

Австралия

Atlantic

Уқёнуси Атлантик

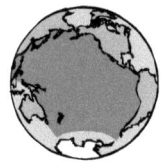

Pacific

Уқёнуси Ором

Indian Ocean

Уқёнуси Ҳинд

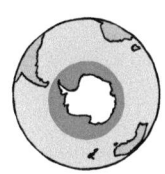

Antarctic Ocean

Уқёнуси Антарктика

Arctic Ocean

Уқёнуси Арктика

North Pole

Қутби шимол

South Pole

Қутби ҷануб

Antarctica

Антарктика

Earth

замин

land

замин

sea

баҳр

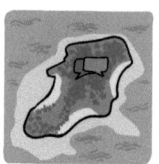

island

ҷазира

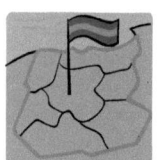

nation

миллат

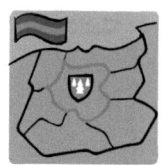

state

давлат

clock face

сиферблат

hour hand

ақрабаки соат

minute hand

ақрабаки дақиқашумор

second hand

ақрабаки сонияшумор

What time is it?

Соат чанд?

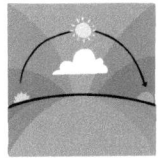

day

рӯз

time

замон

now

ҳозир

digital watch

соати электронӣ

minute

лаҳза

hour

соат

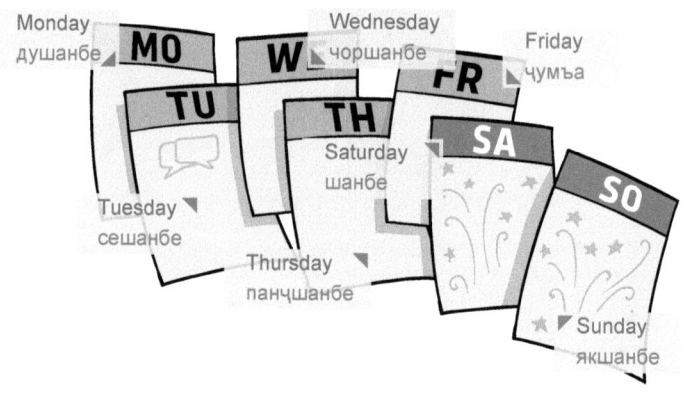

Monday
душанбе

Wednesday
чоршанбе

Friday
ҷумъа

Tuesday
сешанбе

Saturday
шанбе

Thursday
панҷшанбе

Sunday
якшанбе

yesterday

дирӯз

today

имрӯз

tomorrow

фардо

morning

пагоҳирӯзӣ

noon

нимрӯз

evening

шом

business days

рӯзҳои корӣ

weekend

истироҳат

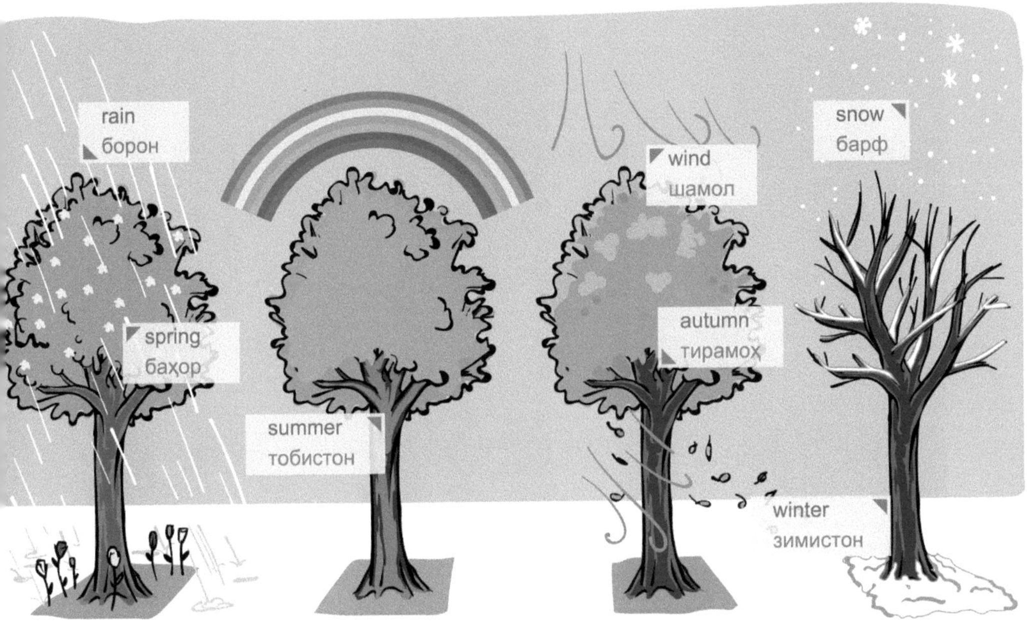

rain
борон

snow
барф

wind
шамол

spring
баҳор

autumn
тирамоҳ

summer
тобистон

winter
зимистон

weather forecast

Обу ҳаво

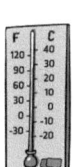

thermometer

ҳароратсанҷ

sunshine

равшании офтоб

cloud

абр

fog

туман

humidity

намнок

lightning

барқ

thunder

тундар

storm

тӯфон

hail

жола

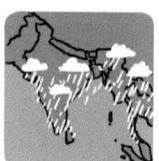

monsoon

муссон

flood

обхезӣ

ice

ях

January

январ

February

феврал

March

март

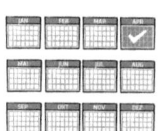

April

апрел

May

май

June

июн

July

июл

August

август

year - сол

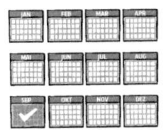

September
....
сентябр

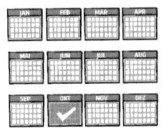

October
....
октябр

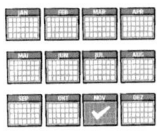

November
....
ноябр

December
....
декабр

shapes
баст

circle
....
давра

square
....
мураббаъ

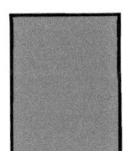

rectangle
....
росткуньа

triangle
....
секуньа

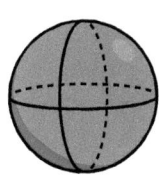

sphere
....
соньаи

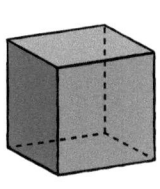

cube
....
мукааб

white
....
гулобӣ

yellow
....
хокистаранг

orange
....
зард

pink
....
бунафшранг

red
....
сурх

purple
....
қаҳваранг

blue
....
кабуд

green
....
сиёҳ

brown
....
кабуд

grey
....
сафед

black
....
сабз

a lot / a little

бисёр/кам

angry / calm

хашмгин / ором

beautiful / ugly

зебо/безеб

beginning / end

оғози / охири

big / small

калон/хурд

bright / dark

дурахшон / торик

brother / sister

бародари / хоҳар

clean / dirty

тоза/чиркин

complete / incomplete

пурра / нопурра

day / night

рӯзи / шаб

dead / alive

мурдагон / зинда

wide / narrow

кушод/танг

edible / inedible

хӯрданӣ / хӯрданашаванда

evil / kind

бад/нек

excited / bored

ба ҳаяҷон / дилгир

fat / thin

ғавс/борик

first / last

якум/охирин

friend / enemy

Дӯсти / душмани

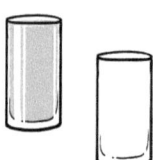

full / empty

пур/холӣ

hard / soft

сахт/мулоим

heavy / light

вазнин/сабук

hunger / thirst

гуруснагӣ / ташнагӣ

ill / healthy

бемор/солим

illegal / legal

ғайриқонунӣ / ҳуқуқӣ

intelligent / stupid

соҳибақл / беақл

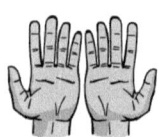

left / right

рост/чап

near / far

наздик/дур

new / used

нави / истифода бурда мешавад

nothing / something

ҳеҷ / чизе

old / young

пир/ҷавон

on / off

оид / хомӯш

open / closed

кушода/пӯшида

quiet / loud

паст/баланд

rich / poor

бой/камбағал

right / wrong

дуруст/нодуруст

rough / smooth

дурушт/ҳамвор

sad / happy

ғамгин/хушбахт

short / long

кӯтоҳ/дароз

slow / fast

оҳиста/тез

wet / dry

тар/хушк

warm / cool

гарм / сард

war / peace

ҷанг / сулҳ

0

zero

нол

1

one

як

2

two

ду

3

three

се

4

four

чор

5

five

панҷ

6

six

шаш

7

seven

ҳафт

8

eight

ҳашт

9

nine

нӯҳ

10

ten

даҳ

11

eleven

ёздаҳ

12

twelve

дувоздаҳ

13

thirteen

сенздаҳ

14

fourteen

чордаҳ

15

fifteen

понздаҳ

16

sixteen

шонздаҳ

17

seventeen

ҳабдаҳ

18

eighteen

ҳаждаҳ

19

nineteen

нуздаҳ

20

twenty

бист

100

hundred

сад

1.000

thousand

ҳазор

1.000.000

million

миллион

English

англисӣ

American English

англисии амрикой

Chinese Mandarin

мандарини хитой

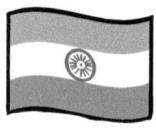

Hindi

ҳиндӣ

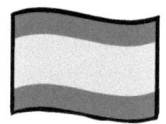

Spanish

испанӣ

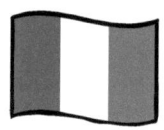

French

фаронсавӣ

Arabic

арабӣ

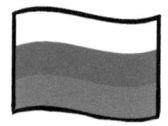

Russian

русӣ

Portuguese

португалӣ

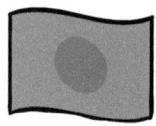

Bengali

бенгалӣ

German

олмонӣ

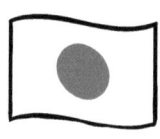

Japanese

ҷопонӣ

I

ман

you

шумо

he / she / it

Ӯ / вай / он

we

мо

you

шумо

they

онҳо

who?

ки?

what?

чй?

how?

Чй хел?

where?

дар кучо?

when?

кай?

name

ном

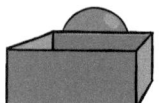

behind

аз паси

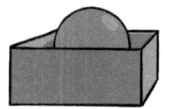

in

дар

in front of

дар пеши

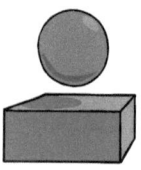

over

дар болои

on

дар рӯи

under

дар зери

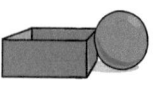

beside

дар назди

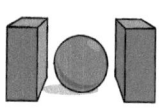

between

миёни

place

чой